Games and Puzzles

for English as a Second Language

Victoria Fremont

and

Brenda Flores

Dover Publications, Inc.
New York

Bibliographical Note

Games and Puzzles for English as a Second Language is a new work, first published by Dover Publications, Inc., in 1995.

International Standard Book Number

ISBN-13: 978-0-486-28468-2
ISBN-10: 0-486-28468-9

Manufactured in the United States by Courier Corporation
28468903   2014
www.doverpublications.com

To all of our students, whose enthusiasm for puzzles inspired us to write this book.

With special thanks to Sister Chantal.

Authors' Note

The puzzles and word games in this volume are an entertaining and engaging way to improve and expand your knowledge of American English. While having fun with these brain-teasing games, you can build vocabulary skills, grammar and usage, and knowledge of common idioms. The material is carefully graded, with the easier puzzles in front, and answers are provided, at the back of the book, for all puzzles. There is a large variety of game types, from crosswords to anagrams, from search-a-word to scrambled word puzzles and homophones. You will find all the puzzles useful and practical, because they emphasize the indispensable, everyday phrases and idioms of contemporary American speech.

Now sharpen your pencils and enjoy!

Connect-a-Color

Can you find the ten colors in this word game? Start with any letter, then move along a black line, in any direction, to another letter until you spell the name of a color. Then write the color names on the lines below. You cannot jump. The first one is done for you.

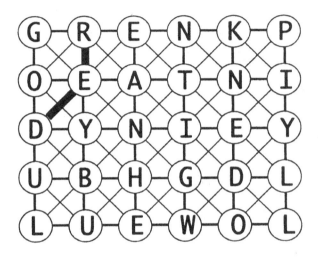

red

Four-Letter Words

Here are 21 common four-letter words. Circle them and write them on the lines below. The first one is done for you. Words go in these directions: ← →   ↕   ↗

```
R  E  T  E  N  T  W  O  N  S
O  D  O  O  R  V  S  I  U  E
O  O  T  M  T  L  A  K  N  L
M  L  A  A  B  R  L  D  L  E
W  L  O  T  O  I  T  E  L  A
T  B  C  R  O  G  P  S  E  F
O  B  L  E  K  F  L  K  B  O
O  X  A  E  B  H  E  A  D  G
F  X  S  T  T  O  O  B  M  W
C  A  C  Y  H  F  O  O  D  P
```

b _ath_____   d _____   l _____

b _____   d _____   r _____

b _____   f _____   r _____

b _____   f _____   s _____

b _____   g _____   s _____

c _____   h _____   t _____

d _____   l _____   t _____

2

Secret Fruits

Pam likes all of these fruits, but the one she likes best is a secret. Fill in the missing letters on each line, and the vertical box will tell you that her favorite fruit is a

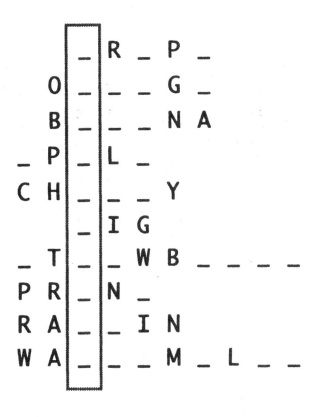

```
      _ R _ P _
  O   _ _ _ G _
  B   _ _ _ N A
_ P   _ L _
C H   _ _ _ Y
      _ I G
_ T   _ _ W B _ _ _ _
P R   _ N _
R A   _ _ I N
W A   _ _ _ M _ L _ _
```

3

Traveling around the United States

Unscramble* each word to find out which states Reiko has visited.

W E N   K R Y O

Ⓞ _ _   _ _ _ _

R O F I L A D

ⓄⓄ _   _ Ⓞ _   _

S T S E H A S A M C U S T

_ _ _ _ ⓄⓄ _ _ _ _ _ _ _

E T X A S

_ _ _ Ⓞ _

A O I A Z R N

_ ⓄⓄ _ Ⓞ _ _

Now, unscramble the letters in the circles, and you'll see that Reiko hasn't seen _____ yet.

*Unscramble: Place the letters in their correct order to make a word.

4

Where Are All the Animals?

Circle these well-known animals and write them on the lines below. The first letter of each animal is given, and the first one is done for you. (Do not include ox.) Words go in these directions: ⟷ ↕ ↗

```
O  E  S  R  O  H  D  R  I  B
E  C  I  D  W  Y  P  L  A  Y
S  A  P  U  L  E  B  I  W  E
U  T  I  G  E  R  L  O  K  K
O  R  G  H  E  N  C  N  C  N
M  A  S  R  A  E  B  E  U  O
Z  E  B  R  A  X  O  F  D  M
G  L  E  M  A  C  E  R  A  T
O  A  T  N  A  H  P  E  L  E
D  N  E  K  C  I  H  C  O  V
```

b _ear_ ___   d _____   m _____

b _____   e _____   o _____

c _____   f _____   p _____

c _____   h _____   r _____

c _____   h _____   s _____

c _____   l _____   t _____

d _____   m _____   z _____

Valeria's Busy Saturday

Valeria had many things to do on Saturday. Fill in each line to see where she went. The vertical box will tell you that her favorite stop is the _____ .

```
D _ _   C | _ | _ _ N _ R
  F L _ _ | _ | S _
          | _ | A _ K
  B _ K _ | _ | Y
      P _ | _ | R M _ _ Y
  S _ P _ | _ | _ _ R _ _ T
B _ _ U _ | _ |   S _ L _ _
```

What's for Lunch?

Circle all the items that are being served in the school cafeteria. The first letter of each word is given, and the first one is done for you. Words go in these directions: ←→ ↕ ↗

```
E  C  I  U  J  H  O  A  H
P  P  L  U  M  S  E  C  H
U  B  R  E  A  D  I  E  S
O  C  A  K  E  W  P  G  I
S  S  F  H  D  Y  O  G  F
S  C  A  N  D  Y  T  S  Y
T  V  A  L  T  O  A  S  T
U  S  O  D  A  E  T  R  E
N  R  O  C  P  D  O  B  X
```

b _read___   j _____   s _____

c _____   n _____   s _____

c _____   p _____   s _____

c _____   p _____   s _____

e _____   p _____   t _____

f _____   p _____   t _____

Verbs in the Past Tense

Try this puzzle of irregular verbs in the past tense.* Using the clues on the facing page, put the missing verbs in the puzzle.

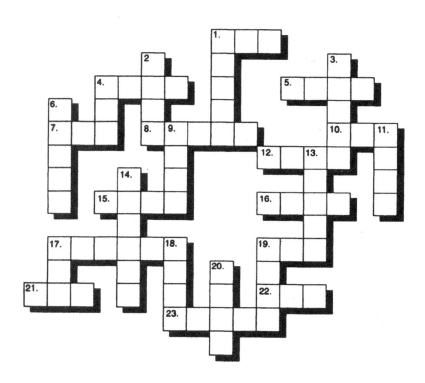

*A regular verb takes the D or ED ending for its past tense, such as *tied* or *walked*. An irregular verb in the past can have the same form as its present, such as *put, put,* or a different form, such as *take, took.*

Verbs in the Past Tense

1. At the horse race Ellen _____ $25 on "Pretty Baby."
4. Yesterday I _____ to the library.
5. Before I bought a new car, I _____ my old one.
7. Last year Ann _____ in the Boston Marathon.
8. Shakespeare _____ *Romeo and Juliet.*
10. When Jesse _____ his hand in his pocket, he found a quarter.
12. I couldn't buy that suit, because it _____ too much.
15. Everyone applauded after the opera singer _____ .
16. The wind _____ Sam's hat off his head.
17. Ted _____ three fish last Saturday.
19. I _____ Karen's parents for the first time yesterday.
21. We _____ dinner at that new restaurant last night.
22. Jane _____ her homework early, so that she could go out.
23. Ben got a speeding ticket, because he _____ too fast.

Down

1. They _____ that beautiful church in the early 1900's.
2. Alice raised her hand since she _____ the answer.
3. I was so tired that I _____ until noon.
4. We were happy when our team _____ the game.
6. When I dropped the glass, it _____ .
9. When the doorbell _____ , our dog started to bark.
11. Joe _____ his pants while he was climbing the fence.
13. The dress was so pretty that Ann _____ all of her money to buy it.
14. The teacher _____ us the irregular verbs.
17. Meg _____ her finger when she was slicing the bread.
18. I'm angry because you _____ a lie.
19. Sue _____ a lot of mistakes on her test last Thursday.
20. Pam _____ photos on her trip to Italy last year.

Common Comparisons

Comparisons are often used in conversations. Can you figure these comparisons out by writing the correct letter in column 2 next to its first part in column 1?

1.	2.
You look very sick; you're _____	a. as stubborn as a mule.
The baby is sleeping; be _____	b. as cold as ice.
Tom got perfect scores on all his exams; he was _____	c. as free as a bird.
Look at Susie all dressed up in her party dress; she looks _____	d. as proud as a peacock.
This bed is very uncomfortable; it's _____	e. as white as a ghost.
Mark will never change his mind; he's _____	f. as hungry as a bear.
I can't see without my glasses; I'm _____	g. as thin as a rail.
Jill hadn't eaten all day; she was _____	h. as fat as a pig.
Ann was so embarrassed when she spilled ink on Bob's shirt; her face turned _____	i. as strong as an ox.
Let's ask Raul to help us move this heavy trunk; he's _____	j. as pretty as a picture.
Akiko went out without her gloves; her hands were _____	k. as old as the hills.
Pablo needs to go on a diet; he's _____	l. as hard as a rock.
I have no responsibilities today; I'm _____	m. as quiet as a mouse.
I've heard that joke a hundred times; it's _____	n. as red as a beet.*
Maria, you need to eat more. You've lost so much weight that you're _____	o. as blind as a bat.

* beet: a dark red vegetable

Crossword of Antonyms

Antonyms are words with opposite meanings, such as *night/day* or *black/white*. Find the antonyms for the words below and put them in the numbered squares.

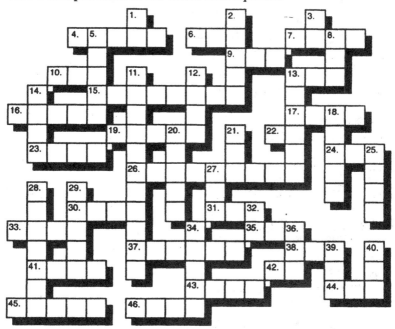

Across

4. over
6. high
7. win
9. answer
10. little
13. good
15. ugly
16. noisy
17. slow
19. always
22. come
23. difficult / hard
24. young
26. cheap
30. first
31. dry
33. early
35. in
37. wide
38. on
41. borrow
42. down
43. far
44. because
45. sour
46. hard

Down

1. she
2. asleep
3. yes
5. day
8. happy
11. boring
12. rich
13. after
14. polite
18. long / tall
20. full
21. hers
25. light
27. old
28. deep
29. dirty
32. from
34. back
36. bottom
39. many
40. sell

Analogies

Find the relationship between the words in the first pair, and then write the word that makes the same relationship in the second pair.

Example: big / little : old / _new_
      large, new, cheap, antique

1. teacher / school : doctor / _____
      sick, hospital, nurse, patient

2. puppy / dog : calf / _____
      cow, kitten, duck, horse

3. eat / ate : drink / _____
      glass, coffee, drunk, drank

4. dime / ten : nickel / _____
      five, money, penny, cents

5. arm / elbow : leg / _____
      toes, knee, body, boot

6. boring / uninteresting : cheap / _____
      costly, sale, buy, inexpensive

7. 'pre' / before : 'post' / _____
      after, often, again, late,

8. strong / weak : dark / _____
      black, heavy, easy, light

9. watch / wrist : ring / _____
      neck, arm, jewelry, finger

10. yellow / lemon : purple / _____
      color, grape, fruit, dark

Analogies

11. vegetable / corn : flower / _____
     beautiful, fruit, bouquet, tulip

12. foot / sock : hand / _____
     glove, shake, arm, thumb

13. cold / freeze : hot / _____
     danger, melt, fire, warm

14. two / pair : twelve / _____
     dozen, eggs, quartet, shoes

15. tea / cup : soup / _____
     liquid, chicken, bowl, plate

16. wide / long : width / _____
     height, length, tall, depth

17. one / won : two / _____
     three, too, game, lost

18. laugh / cry : smile / _____
     whisper, cough, frown, happy

19. pen / paper : chalk / _____
     eraser, notebook, pencil, blackboard

20. newspaper / read : television / _____
     radio, watch, study, talk

21. man / men : tooth / _____
     teeth, face, dentist, mouth

22. on / off : top / _____
     under, over, bottom, inside

What the Thief Stole!

Each scrambled word below is something valuable, like jewelry or expensive furniture. Unscramble* each word to find out what the thief stole.

A C K N L E C E

_ OO _ _ _ _ __

C T A H W

_ O _ _ _

E O Y M N

O _ _ _ _

G I T A N N P I

_ O _ _ _ _ _ _

I R G N

O _ _ _

Now take the letters in the circles and unscramble them. The thief forgot to steal the expensive _____.

Unscramble: Place the letters in their correct order to make a word.

Clothing

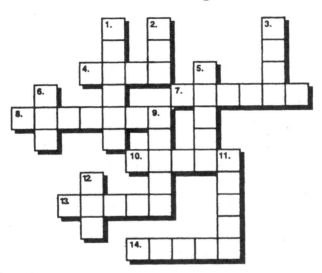

Across

4.

7.

8.

10.

13.

14.

Down

1.

2.

3.

5.

6.

9.

11.

12.

He's Really a Pain in the Neck!

This expression using a part of the body means that someone really gets on your nerves. Here are more common expressions using parts of the body. Read each sentence and put the letter of its definition (under Answers) on the line. (Try not to use a dictionary.)

You've reminded me about it six times! Now *get off my back!* I don't want to hear it again. _____

Before a performer goes on stage, his friends often say, *"Break a leg!"* _____

He wasn't telling me the truth. I could *feel it in my bones.* _____

Gee, Mom, I didn't really pay $200 for this baseball card. I was just *pulling your leg.* _____

You already have two fur coats! You need another one *like you need a hole in the head.* _____

I'm sure you can solve this problem. You *have a good head on your shoulders.* _____

They don't *see eye to eye* on politics. He's much more conservative than she is. _____

Have a heart! Don't give us so much homework. It's the weekend! _____

I'd like to remodel my kitchen, but it would *cost an arm and a leg!* _____

My sister said she'd *keep an eye on* our house while we're on vacation. She's going to pick up the mail and water the plants. _____

I'm angry with Mary for being so *nosy.* She opened one of my letters! _____

He's Really a Pain in the Neck!

I'm *up to my ears* in work. I don't know how I'll ever finish this by Tuesday. _____

It was so frustrating. The answer was *on the tip of my tongue*, but I just couldn't say it. _____

I'm not sure how much money we've made. But *off the top of my head*, I'd say about $1500. _____

Keep your chin up! I'm sure you'll find a job soon. _____

Tell me everything that happened. I'm *all ears*. _____

Bite your tongue! It is *not* going to rain on the day of the picnic. _____

Answers

a. Know by instinct.

b. Be compassionate. Show mercy.

c. Be extremely expensive.

d. Think logically.

e. Have the same point of view.

f. Have an overwhelming amount.

g. Can't wait to hear the news.

h. A first reaction without giving it much thought.

i. Good luck.

j. Can *almost* remember something.

k. Be careful what you say; it may not be what we want to hear.

l. Don't get discouraged or lose hope.

m. Just joking, kidding.

n. Overly interested in someone else's personal matters.

o. Watch something for someone else.

p. Leave me alone. Don't bother me!

q. You don't need this at all.

Searching for Irregular Past Participles

Look at the 26 verbs on the next page and find their irregular past participles in this puzzle.* Circle each one and write it next to its present and past form. The first one is done for you. Words go in these directions: ←→ ↕ ↗

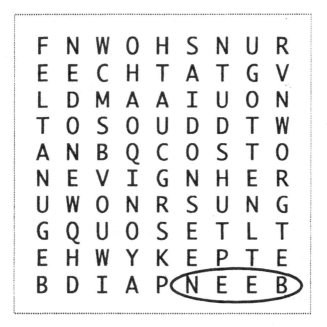

```
F  N  W  O  H  S  N  U  R
E  E  C  H  T  A  T  G  V
L  D  M  A  A  I  U  O  N
T  O  S  O  U  D  D  T  W
A  N  B  Q  C  O  S  T  O
N  E  V  I  G  N  H  E  R
U  W  O  N  R  S  U  N  G
G  Q  U  O  S  E  T  L  T
E  H  W  Y  K  E  P  T  E
B  D  I  A  P  N  E  E  B
```

*Past participles are used with the auxiliary verb *to have.* **Regular** past participles are formed by adding D or ED, as in *he has died* or *he has finished.* An **irregular** past participle may be the same as its present form, as in *I put, I have put,* or different from its present form, as in *I feel, I have felt* or *I go, I have gone.*

Searching for Irregular Past Participles

Am, Was, _been_

Begin, Began, _____

Bet, Bet, _____

Come, Came, _____

Cost, Cost, _____

Dig, Dug, _____

Do, Did, _____

Feel, Felt, _____

Get, Got, _____

Give, Gave, _____

Grow, Grew, _____

Hang, Hung, _____

Have, Had, _____

Keep, Kept, _____

Pay, Paid, _____

Quit, Quit, _____

Run, Ran _____

Say, Said, _____

See, Saw, _____

Set, Set, _____

Show, Showed, _____

Shut, Shut, _____

Sing, Sang, _____

Sit, Sat, _____

Wear, Wore, _____

Win, Won, _____

In the Kitchen

Jurgen just moved into his new apartment. His kitchen was great, but he needed to buy a small appliance. Unscramble* each word to see what was in his kitchen.

N S K I

$\underline{\text{O}}$ _ _ _

S H E R A W D I H S

_ _ _ _ _ $\underline{\text{O}}$ _ _ _ $\underline{\text{O}}$

O E V S T

_ $\underline{\text{O}}$ _ _ _

A T G E R R I F E R O R

_ $\underline{\text{O}}$ _ _ _ _ _ _ $\underline{\text{O}}$ _

A C N   R E N P E O

_ _ _ $\underline{\text{O}}$ _ _ _ _ _

Now, unscramble the letters in the circles, and you'll see that he's going to buy a _____.

Unscramble: Place the letters in their correct order to make a word.

Missing Animals

Put a letter in each blank square so that each numbered column
(↓) makes a three-letter word and the center, horizontal line
(→) spells the name of a familiar farm animal.

	1	2	3	4	5	6	7
↓	A	T	S	I	S	M	E
→	C				K		
	T	E	T	E	Y	N	D

This one spells the name of a familiar jungle animal.

	1	2	3	4	5	6	7
↓	A	T	S	A	M	C	A
→	L			P			
	L	N	N	E	P	Y	D

College Courses

Can you find the 15 courses that Jean has taken at the university? Circle them and write them on the lines below. The first letter of each subject is given, and the first one is done for you. Words go in these directions: ←→ ↕ ↗

```
H T A M C I S U M U
P H I L O S O P H Y
H T Y R O T S I H E
Y O L A T I N P Y H
S U D R A M A G H T
I L A W F R E N C H
C L E N G L I S H M
S E C O N O M I C S
C H E M I S T R Y I
V G H H S I N A P S
```

A _rt_____   F _____   M _____

C _____   G _____   M _____

D _____   H _____   P _____

E _____   L _____   P _____

E _____   L _____   S _____

22

Homophones

A homophone is a word having the same sound as another word but having a different meaning and spelling, such as *too/two* or *here/hear*. Try this puzzle to see how many homophones you know.

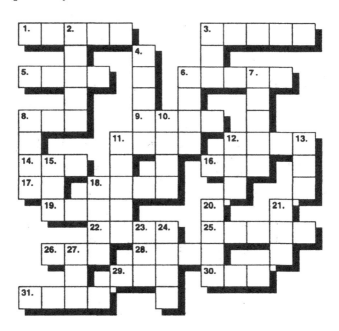

Across

1. plain
3. hole
5. rows
6. nose
8. lye
9. shoo
11. beat
12. blue
14. eight
16. read
17. dew
18. male
19. week
22. deer
25. allowed
26. die
28. role
29. see
30. I
31. you're

Down

2. I'll
3. one
4. rays
6. not
7. wood
8. led
10. heel
11. break
12. be
13. weigh
15. toe
18. maid
20. tail
21. by
23. R
24. rode
27. U

Packing for Her Trip

Marie packed all of these clothes for her trip to England, but she forgot one important thing. Fill in the missing letters on each line, and the vertical box will tell you that she forgot to take her _____ .

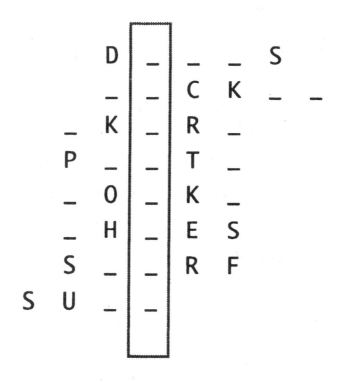

Let's Travel

Circle the words that relate to travel and write them on the lines below. The first letter of each word is given, and the first one is done for you. Words go in these directions: ← → ↕ ↗

```
N  O  I  T  A  V  R  E  S  E  R
T  S  M  S  P  V  Y  B  K  T  G
R  U  I  I  F  L  O  C  E  E  D
A  I  L  G  F  A  A  K  X  L  A
I  T  E  H  T  P  C  N  H  U  O
N  C  T  T  G  I  M  O  E  D  R
N  A  O  S  T  A  T  I  P  E  L
S  S  U  E  P  E  C  A  R  H  L
U  E  R  E  L  I  X  A  T  C  I
B  K  S  T  A  T  I  O  N  S  B
```

b _ill_____   m _____   s _____

b _____   p _____   s _____

b _____   p _____   t _____

c _____   r _____   t _____

f _____   r _____   t _____

h _____   s _____   t _____

m _____   s _____   t _____

Oscar's Living Room

Oscar likes all of these things in his living room, but there's something in the living room that he likes best. Unscramble* each of the following words.

C I U T E R S P

_ _ Ⓞ _ _ Ⓞ _ _

O S T R E E

_ _ Ⓞ _ _ _

S L O N E T I E V I

_ Ⓞ _ _ _ _ _ Ⓞ _ _

A F O S

_ _ ⓄⓄ

P A L M

Ⓞ _ _ Ⓞ

Now, unscramble the letters in the circles and you'll see that he likes the_____ the most.

Unscramble: Place the letters in their correct order to make a word.

More Homophones

A homophone is a word having the same sound as another word but having a different meaning and spelling, such as *too/two* or *here/hear*. Try this puzzle to see how many homophones you know.

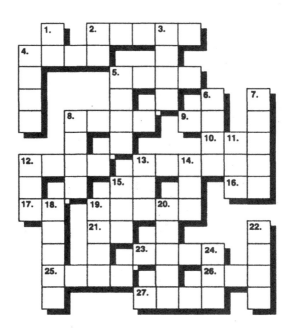

Across

2. bares
4. sighs
5. pale
8. weight
9. inn
10. won
12. tide
13. flour
15. sew
16. wee
17. oar
19. hoarse
21. Anne
23. meet
25. higher
26. I
27. flee

Down

1. high
2. bee
3. reign
4. sail
5. pear
6. no
7. their
8. we'd
11. knew
12. too
13. four
14. oh
15. sun
18. write
19. hare
20. steel
22. blue
24. tee

Setting the Table

Amy was so excited on her birthday that while she was setting the table she forgot something. Unscramble* each word to see what Amy has put on the table.

LESTAP

_ _ O _ _ _

VIKENS

_ OO _ _ _

PONSOS

_ O _ _ O _

WOLSB

_ _ _ _ O

RSOFK

_ _ _ O _

Now, unscramble the letters in the circles, and you'll see that Amy forgot the _____.

*Unscramble: Place the letters in their correct order to make a word.

Parts of the Body

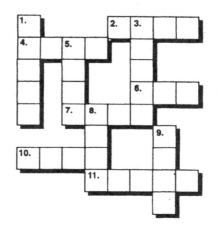

10. across

2. across

5. down

11. across

9. down

3. down

8. down

4. across

1. down

6. across

7. across

He Has the Memory of an Elephant!

This expression using an animal means that someone has an excellent memory. Here are more common expressions using animals. Read each sentence and put the letter of its definition (under Answers) on the line. (Try not to use a dictionary.)

John wasn't surprised at his surprise party, because Sue *let the cat out of the bag.* ____

Jack was about to marry Jane, but at the last minute he *chickened out.* ____

When I introduced myself to the new student, he hardly talked to me. What *a cold fish!* ____

Will you stop telling me to clean up my room? I heard you the first time. *Don't bug me!* ____

When Joe was in college he loved to drink a lot and stay out late at all the parties. He was really *a party animal!* ____

When Ann and Beth spent the weekend together, they went off their diets and *pigged out* on pizza, coke and candy. ____

Don't forget your umbrella. It's *raining cats and dogs.* ____

The salesman told me that this was the best buy! But I found out I could buy the same thing at a much lower price. I *outfoxed* him! ____

Holy cow! Did you see how fast that horse ran! He won the race by a mile! ____

Paul is married and has a girlfriend. What *a rat!* ____

Relax! We won't be late. *Hold your horses!* ____

Jason got an apartment on the thirtieth floor. He has *a bird's-eye view* of the park. ____

He Has the Memory of an Elephant!

Whenever I have to speak in front of a large group of people, I get *butter-flies in my stomach.* ____

John told me that he had found three hundred dollars in the street. That's *a fishy story!* ____

Bill and Beth were very hungry, but they had to finish a project. They *killed two birds with one stone* by working on the project at dinner. ____

Sue is going to tell her boss that she is going to quit. I'd like to be *a fly on the wall* when that happens! ____

Answers

a. Difficult to believe.

b. A good view from high above.

c. Tell a secret.

d. Able to overhear something.

e. An unfriendly person.

f. That's amazing!

g. Have more patience.

h. It's very wet outside, pouring.

i. Get nervous.

j. Stop annoying me!

k. Get scared and change one's mind.

l. He was sure he was smart, but I was smarter.

m. A dishonest or unethical person.

n. Get two things done at one time.

o. Eat a lot of food at one time (usually low in nutrition).

p. Someone who attends too many parties.

Chantal's Vegetable Garden

Chantal loves vegetables and grows all of these in her garden.
Unscramble* each word to find out what they are.

E E T T L C U

_ _ _ O _ _ _

Y R C L E E

O _ _ _ O _

O A P T T O E S

_ _ _ O _ _ _ _

A E P S

_ _ _ O

S U M H O R M S O

_ _ _ _ O O _ _

Now, unscramble the letters in the circles, and you'll see that
_____ are her favorite.

Unscramble: Place the letters in their correct order to make a word.

Sports, Sports, Sports

Here are 21 sports-related words for you to circle. The first letter of each word is given, and the first one is done for you. Words go in these directions: ←→ ↕ ↗

```
H C T I P I T E B S R
O K C A R T S S A C A
N G O L F O I U T O C
V U E R L N G N N R E
B T R R N X F I I E F
A E G E R I B F O D P
S K T O E O Q O P W K
E C Y L A N R R T I H
U A D B A L L M C N Z
I R V L U O F K B E P
```

b <u>all</u>   g _____   r _____

b _____   h _____   r _____

b _____   k _____   s _____

e _____   l _____   t _____

f _____   p _____   t _____

f _____   p _____   u _____

g _____   r _____   w _____

The Car

Marcello bought a used car. Unscramble* each word to find out what parts of the car didn't have to be fixed.

S I A H G L E D H T

_ _ _ _ O _ _ O _

E W H E S L

_ _ O _ _ O

I W E P R S

_ _ _ O _ _

R U T K N

O _ _ _ _

A K E R B S

O _ O _ _ _

Now, unscramble the letters in the circles, and you'll see that the _____ was broken.

*Unscramble: Place the letters in their correct order to make a word.

Match the Idiom

Here are 16 well-known idioms or expressions. Can you figure them out? Write the letter of the second part of the idiom next to its first part. The first one is done for you.

A bird in the hand ___k___   a. is golden.

Two is company, _____   b. is the mother of invention.

Better late _____   c. as you'd have them do unto you.

You can lead a horse to water _____ d. is through his stomach.

Necessity _____   e. but you can't make it drink.

All things come _____   f. three is a crowd.

Don't count your chickens _____   g. to forgive divine.

The love of money _____   h. are soon parted.

The way to a man's heart _____   i. to those who wait.

Silence _____   j. over spilled milk.

Don't cry _____   k. is worth two in the bush.

Do unto others _____   l. is not gold.

A fool and his money _____   m. is the root of all evil.

A stitch in time _____   n. than never.

All that glitters _____   o. saves nine.

To err is human, _____   p. before they're hatched.

What's My Job?

Try this crossword puzzle of occupations using the clues on the facing page.

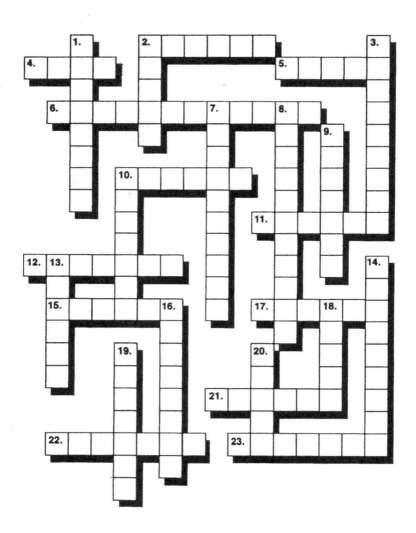

What's My Job?

Across

2. We arrest criminals and protect your community.
4. I cook the food in restaurants.
5. I play different roles in movies or on TV.
6. I use a camera to do my job.
10. When you are sick, you see me.
11. I paint, draw, or make things from clay.
12. I sell flowers and plants.
15. I serve food in a restaurant.
17. I cut men's hair.
21. I grow food and raise animals.
22. You call me when there is a problem with the water pipes.
23. I help students learn.

Down

1. I repair automobiles.
2. I fly airplanes.
3. I design houses and other buildings.
7. I keep track of financial records and prepare your taxes.
8. I install and repair electrical wiring in your house.
9. I run the cash register in a store or a restaurant.
10. When you have a toothache, you call me.
13. I give you legal advice.
14. I build things out of wood.
16. I write stories in your newspaper.
18. I'm the person who makes bread and cake.
19. If there's a fire in your house, call me.
20. I take care of patients and work with doctors.

Secret Language

Yasin can speak ten languages, but there's one he hasn't studied yet. Fill in the missing letters on each line to find out the languages he knows. The vertical box will tell you that he still wants to study _____ .

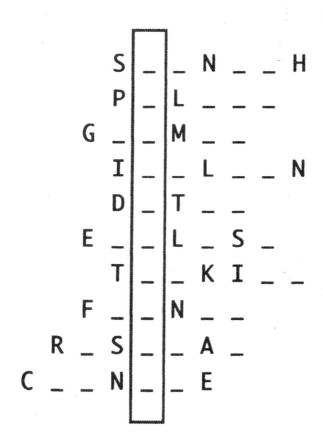

```
        S  _  _  N  _  _  H
        P  _  L  _  _  _
     G  _  _  M  _  _
        I  _  _  L  _  _  N
        D  _  T  _  _
     E  _  _  L  _  S  _
        T  _  _  K  I  _  _
     F  _  _  N  _  _
   R  _  S  _  _  A  _
 C  _  _  N  _  _  E
```

Things to Do

Here are 21 different activities for you to circle. They're all verbs (do not include hop or go), and the first one is done for you. Words go in these directions: ←→ ↕ ↗

H S I F T I N K V
E V I R D K R O W
S I N G P Z D S A
T Y E T R A V E L
G D F D E U I W K
O U D R A T N N X
J T R I B N I B T
B S A K O O C R F
M I W S H O P E W

draw _____ _____

_____ _____ _____

_____ _____ _____

_____ _____ _____

_____ _____ _____

_____ _____ _____

_____ _____ _____

The Drugstore

Unscramble* each word to find out what Morio bought at the drugstore.

N I S P A R I

○_ ○_ _ _ _ _

H A S P M O O

○○_ _ _ _ _ ○

I C E M D I N E

_ _ _ _ _ _ _ ○

T A N V I M I S

_ _ ○_ _ _ _ _

O O R U B H S T H T

○○_ ○_ _ _ _ _ _

Now, unscramble the letters in the circles and you'll see that Morio forgot to buy _____

*Unscramble: Place the letters in their correct order to make a word.

40

Connect an Irregular Verb

There are 17 IRREGULAR verbs in the PAST tense in this puzzle.*   Start with any letter, then move along a black line, in any direction, to find each verb.   You cannot jump.   (Hint: six of the irregular verbs begin with the letter S).   The first one is done for you.

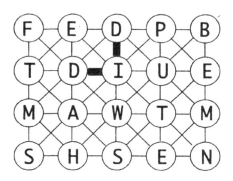

did _____   _____   _____

_____   _____   _____

_____   _____   _____

_____   _____   _____

_____   _____   _____

_____   _____   _____

*A regular verb takes the D or ED ending for its past tense, such as *tied* or *walked*. An irregular verb in the past can have the same form as its present, such as *cut, cut* or a different form, such as *sing, sang*.

All He Bought for Christmas

Circle the 24 Christmas presents on Mr. Money's list. The first letter of each word is given, and the first one is done for you. Words go in these directions: ←→ ↕ ↗

```
B  M  I  R  A  D  I  O  R  E
J  U  K  O  O  B  T  P  I  M
E  G  C  L  S  B  A  D  N  U
W  E  L  Z  Z  U  P  L  G  F
E  A  O  G  A  M  E  B  L  R
L  R  T  R  I  H  S  I  O  E
R  O  H  C  L  O  C  K  V  P
Y  B  E  S  H  A  T  E  E  E
V  E  S  K  A  T  E  S  S  N
```

b _at_____   g _____   r _____

b _____   h _____   r _____

b _____   j _____   s _____

b _____   m _____   s _____

c _____   p _____   t _____

c _____   p _____   t _____

d _____   p _____   t _____

g _____   r _____   w _____

Answers

p. 1 Colors

red	orange
blue	tan
green	pink
yellow	gray (grey)
white	gold

p. 2 Four-Letter Words

p. 3 Secret Fruits

grape	fig
orange	strawberry
banana	prune
apple	raisin
cherry	watermelon

secret word = grapefruit

p. 4 Traveling

New York
Florida
Massachusetts

Texas
Arizona
missing word = California

p. 5 Animals

p. 6 Busy Saturday

dry cleaner
florist
bank
bakery

pharmacy
supermarket
beauty salon
secret word = library

p. 7 Lunch

pp. 8-9 Past Tense

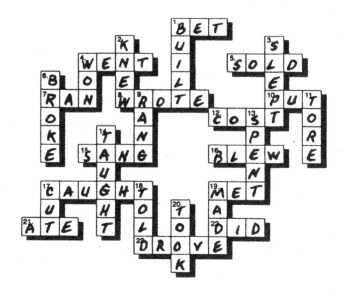

p. 10 Comparisons

You look very sick; you're (e)

The baby is sleeping; be (m)

Tom got perfect scores on all his exams; he was (d)

Look at Susie all dressed up in her party dress; she looks (j)

This bed is very uncomfortable; it's (l)

Mark will never change his mind; he's (a)

I can't see without my glasses; I'm (o)

Jill hadn't eaten all day; she was (f)

Ann was so embarrassed when she spilled ink on Bob's shirt;
    her face turned (n)

Let's ask Raul to help us move this heavy trunk; he's (i)

Akiko went out without her gloves; her hands were (b)

Pablo needs to go on a diet; he's (h)

I have no responsibilities today; I'm (c)

I've heard that joke a hundred times; it's (k)

Maria, you need to eat more. You've lost so much weight that you're (g)

p. 11 Antonyms

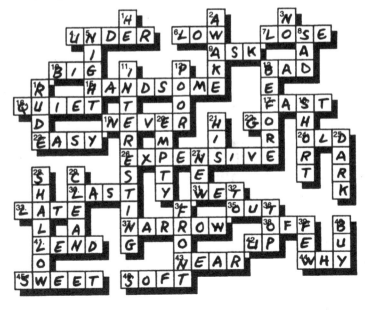

pp. 12-13 Analogies

1. hospital
2. cow
3. drank
4. five
5. knee
6. inexpensive
7. after
8. light
9. finger
10. grape
11. tulip
12. glove
13. melt
14. dozen
15. bowl
16. length
17. too
18. frown
19. blackboard
20. watch
21. teeth
22. bottom

p. 14 Thief

necklace
watch
money

painting
ring
missing word = camera

p. 15 Clothing

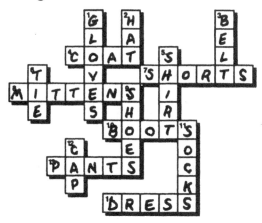

pp. 16-17 Pain in the Neck

get off my back (p)

break a leg (i)

feel it in my bones (a)

pulling your leg (m)

like you need a hole
  in the head (q)

have a good head
  on your shoulders (d)

see eye to eye (e)

have a heart (b)

cost an arm and a leg (c)

keep an eye on (o)

nosy (n)

up to my ears ((f)

on the tip of my tongue (j)

off the top of my head (h)

keep your chin up (l)

all ears (g)

bite your tongue (k)

pp. 18-19 Past Participles

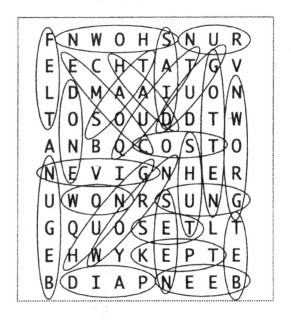

p. 20 Kitchen

sink
dishwasher
stove

refrigerator
can opener
missing word = toaster

p. 21 Missing Animals

chicken · leopard

p. 22 College Courses

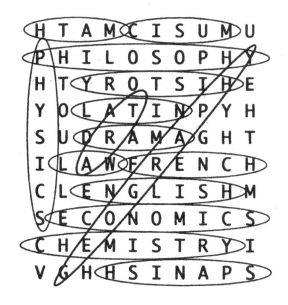

p. 23 Homophones

p. 24 Packing

dress
jacket
skirt
pants
socks
shoes
scarf
suit
secret word = raincoat

p. 25 Let's Travel

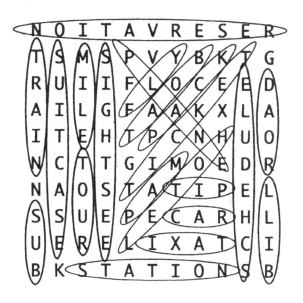

p. 26 Living Room

pictures
stereo
television
sofa
lamp
missing word = fireplace

p. 27 More Homophones

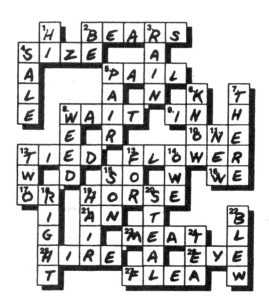

p. 28 Setting the Table

plates
knives
spoons
bowls
forks
missing word = napkins

p. 29 Parts of the Body

pp. 30-31 Memory of an Elephant

let the cat out of the bag (c)
chickened out (k)
a cold fish (e)
don't bug me (j)
a party animal (p)
pigged out (o)
raining cats and dogs (h)
outfoxed (l)
holy cow (f)
a rat (m)
hold your horses (g)
bird's-eye view (b)
butterflies in my stomach (i)
a fishy story (a)
kill two birds with one stone (n)
a fly on the wall (d)

p. 32 Vegetable Garden

lettuce
celery
potatoes
peas
mushrooms
missing word = carrots

p. 33 Sports

p. 34 Car

headlights
wheels
wipers
trunk
brakes
missing word = seatbelt

p. 35 Match the Idiom

A bird in the hand (k)
Two is company (f)
Better late (n)
You can lead a horse to water (e)
Necessity (b)
All things come (i)
Don't count your chickens (p)
The love of money (m)

The way to a man's heart (d)
Silence (a)
Don't cry (j)
Do unto others (c)
A fool and his money (h)
A stitch in time (o)
All that glitters (l)
To err is human (g)

pp. 36-37 Jobs

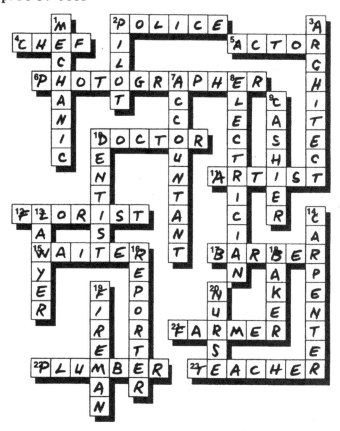

p. 38 Secret Language

Spanish
Polish
German
Italian
Dutch
English
Turkish
French
Russian
Chinese
secret word = Portuguese

p. 39 Things to Do

p. 40 Drugstore

aspirin
shampoo
medicine
vitamins
toothbrush
missing word = toothpaste

p. 41 Connect an Irregular Verb

did	met	set
ate	put	swam
bet	said	was
fed	sat	went
had	saw	wet
made	sent	

p. 42 Christmas

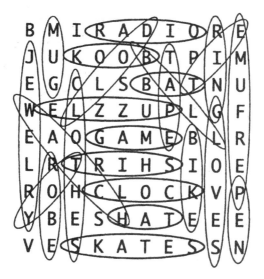